Tapestry of Secrets

poems by

Carol Alena Aronoff, Ph.D.

Finishing Line Press
Georgetown, Kentucky

Tapestry of Secrets

Copyright © 2019 by Carol Alena Aronoff, Ph.D.
ISBN 978-1-64662-079-1 First Edition
All rights reserved under International and Pan-American Copyright Conventions. No part of this book may be reproduced in any manner whatsoever without written permission from the publisher, except in the case of brief quotations embodied in critical articles and reviews.

ACKNOWLEDGMENTS

I would like to thank the editors of the following publications for including some of my poems:

Secrets and Dreams Anthology: In the Shadows
Bearing the Mask: Southwestern Persona Poems: Los Secretos de Mi Abuelita, Remembering Mi Abuelo, Kaddish (nominated for the Pushcart Prize)
Otherwise Engaged: En las Manos de Dio

Publisher: Leah Maines
Editor: Christen Kincaid
Cover Art: Photograph of a wood carving, *Guadalupana* by Richard D. Romero
Author Photo: Dixon Enos
Cover Design: Elizabeth Maines McCleavy

Printed in the USA on acid-free paper.
Order online: www.finishinglinepress.com
also available on amazon.com

Author inquiries and mail orders:
Finishing Line Press
P. O. Box 1626
Georgetown, Kentucky 40324
U. S. A.

Table of Contents

Los Secretos de Mi Abuelita 1

Recipe for Disaster 2

Convento de Santo Domingo Pueblo 3

In the Shadows 4

En las Manos de Dio 5

Love Letters 6

Seeking Refuge 7

The Interpreter 9

Pirate, Rabbi, Diplomat, Spy 11

Double Wedding 13

Sub Rosa 14

Los Marranos 15

When to Do Nothing 17

Autumn Sabbath 18

Unborn Reveries 19

The Birth 20

Remembering Mi Abuelo 21

Prayers to Be Inscribed in the Book of Life for another Year 22

Kaddish 23

Cara Vemos, Corazón no Concemos 25

Suggested Readings 26

For the courageous and creative generations of conversos/crypto-Jews and their descendants who arrived in New Mexico originally from Spain or Portugal to avoid the Inquisition, carrying on their traditions in secret and at great risk.

Los Secretos de Mi Abuelita

From a low branch, I watch
Abuelita's house as the sun
disappears on a Friday. Soft light
flickers behind closed curtains.

I want to ask about just lit candles,
the bowl of water and herbs in her room
near a *retablo* of *Santa Esterika*,
what she and *Madrecita* use it for
each month. Some secrets ennoble
their guardians, others speak from dark
closets in language we no longer understand.

Why do we clean on Fridays, stop at sunset,
not wear yellow? Lines in *Abuelita's* face
are sculpted by what is hidden. Veiling
her true heart, devotion to *El Dio*: exhaustion—
the strain of keeping a gourd from breaking
into a thousand pieces, of knowing whether
to let the unrevealed be buried with her or pass
along the joy and burden to another generation.

Which road to follow when none is marked
by safety and the only certainty is risk?
The weight of our ancestral soul map.
Standing vigil next to fields of corn and squash,
the ordinariness of white sheets and petticoats
on a clothesline lend cover to any cracks
in her *fachada*. I ask her why I love Santo Moises
but don't like going to church. *Esta en la sangre,
pobrecita*, is all she will say.

Los Secretos de Mi Abuelita (Sp)—My Grandma's Secrets
Abuelita (Sp)—grandma
retablo (Sp)—religious painting on wood or metal
Madrecita (Sp)—little mother, term of endearment
El Dio (Sp)—God
fachada (Sp)—facade
Esta en la sangre, pobrecita (Sp)—It's in the blood, poor little one

Recipe for Disaster

Take one priest walking by
our open window who has read
the recipes in the *Regimento
de Inquisition General* to ferret out
Judaizers and has a sharp sense
of smell.

Place *Abuelita* in the kitchen
preparing food for semana santa
(*Pesah* to us): *pan de semita, lentejas,
huevos haminados* and my favorite,
capirotada, the bread pudding
priests especially look out for.

Add layers of stale bread, raisins,
dried fruit, cinnamon syrup, cloves,
cheese and nuts baked together with
grandmother's weather-veined hands.
Heavenly smells that can give us away
and lead us to hell.

I ask *Abuelita* how something
so delicious could be deadly,
how what we eat could matter
to anyone but ourselves. *There is
poison in small minds even when
the belly is full*, she sighs.

Regimento de Inquisition General (Sp)—book printed in 1640 that gave detailed instructions on how to search for fake converts from Judaism to Catholicism.
Judaizers (Gr)—*conversos* secretly practicing their old faith
semana santa (Sp)—Holy Week
Pesah (Heb)—Passover
pan de semita (Sp)—Semitic bread eaten around Passover and Lent
lentejas (Sp)—lentil soup
huevos haminados (Sp)—eggs hard-boiled with onion skins
capirotada (Sp)—bread pudding

Convento de Santo Domingo Pueblo

From her prison cell
Tia Ana dreams of sky
        unobstructed:

Six-pointed stars
form ancient constellations,
        shine proud
yet invisible to an Inquisitor's eye.

In the far away,
        Sangre de Cristo
dressed in purple velvet
with ornaments of silver sage.

On the roof of my adobe,
        an oud player
sings old Sephardic ballads
        heard only
by those who keep
        the secret.

In this dream,
        she flies free.
No masks conceal her true face.
She looks in a mirror,
        sees she is still lit
from within.

Tia (Sp)—aunt
Sangre de Cristo (Sp)—(blood of Christ), mountain range in N. New Mexico and S. Colorado

In the Shadows

Night rises from embers
of sun-dyed canyons,
nods to the last amber
glow in the west
and settles in to fill small
hours with songs
of triumph and darkest loss.

I am a singer in this chorus
of shadows. Dreaming
in palettes of indigo and gray,
I find myself searching
for clarity and color. For stones'
glow, familial secrets,
for the heart of firefly.

Dropping down a well
in this cave of the self,
I come upon ghosts
and pot sherds: signs of lost
tribes fleeing, of broken promises
and hidden rites I carry without
knowing. A *Magen David*, pale

specter on these walls, I remember
from the side of an old gravestone
down the San Luis valley where
ancestors etched crosses and false
names for safety. And *mi abuelita*
sang the *Sh'ma* so softly in language
I knew only in my soul.

Magen David (Heb)—Star of David
Sh'ma (Heb)—important Jewish prayer

En las Manos de Dio

Your hand, a whisper on the bed
arrayed for *la muerte*, your frail fingers,
musical notes you sang to comfort me.

I kiss each finger and pray
your songs will last forever.
But only moon's memories will linger.

My breathing seems too loud for the room,
too coarse and ragged for your small cloud
form. Too alive.

You are still, your body disappeared
into dream. I will dream along with you
for as long as life will hold you.

I have loved you fierce, *Abuelita*, loved
your hands enfolding mine like nesting
dolls, loved your plaited mysteries.

Your long hair in ivory combs, silver brooches,
the way you kissed your fingers and touched
the crucifix by your door. So much left unspoken.

I turn you on your side facing the wall
and hear your voice for the last time,
Su bisabuela fue una conversa.

En las Manos de Dio (Sp)—In God's Hands
la muerte (Sp)—death
Su bisabuela fue una conversa (Sp)—Your great-grandmother was a convert

Love Letters

Mi abuelo says that stories are
well-loved children who grow taller
with the years. We must savor them
like favorite sweets and share them
with our own children when we are old.

One night, I overhear him tell *mi padre*
of *El Illuminado's* pears—Luis de Carvajal
in prison with his mother and sisters
for practicing our faith. His love of
El Dio and *la familia* so strong, he sent

messages of blessing and encouragement,
*Have patience like Job; may Adonay, our Lord,
visit you*, on the pit of an alligator pear
wrapped in taffeta, hidden inside a melon
for the warden to give to his sister Leonor.

Each day he scratched notes on fruit
which the warden passed on to Inquisitors.
They say Luis knew that would happen
but never wavered, his *emunah*
stronger than any fear for his life.

For this he burned.

---

mi abuelo (Sp)—my grandfather
mi padre (Sp)—my father
El Illuminado (Sp)—(The Enlightened One), Luis de Carvajal
la familia (Sp)—the family
Adonay (Heb)—Lord
emunah (Heb)—faith

Seeking Refuge

> *Surely the isles shall wait for me, and the ships of Tarshish first, to bring thy sons from far, their silver and their gold with them, Book of Isaiah, 60:9, cited by Columbus in his writings.*

I run away from sleep on nights
when *mi padre, mi abuelo y mis tios*
sit at the table and talk. Pass
along the teachings they recall.

Tell stories of *el pasado distante*
to keep our heroes and warriors,
mostly in Christian guise, alive.
To remember.

My head swims with tales
of caravels, cartographers,
conquistadors and cities
for conversos.

I hear *Tio* Luis mention
Cristovao Colon—*reyacha*,
he says, who sailed from Spain
with a promise, and a secret
mission to find the Lost Tribes.

Fasting for *Tisha B'av*, he set out
next day as the Edict of Expulsion
took effect. His origins and true name
a mystery, his destination also uncertain.

Was he Salvador Fernandes Zarco
of Cuba, Portugal seeking refuge for Jews
in the new world? *Mi tio* says that in letters
to his son Diego, Colon used a cabbalistic

signet like those inscribed on Jewish graves
and the two Hebrew letters for *B'Ezrat HaShem*,

with God's help. *Abuelo* says he wanted gold
to liberate Jerusalem, rebuild the Holy Temple.

Listening to these *historias* I wish sometimes
I could stow away and sail, a wandering Jew,
to a place without Inquisitors or the threat
of *autos de fe*, a place of no sorrow.

---

mi tios (Sp)—my uncles
el pasado distante (Sp)—the distant past
reyacha (Heb)—fellow Jew
Tisha B'av (Heb)—day of mourning the destruction of the first and second Holy Temples in Jerusalem
historias (Sp)—stories
autos de fe (Sp)—(acts of faith), Inquisition rites of denunciation and burning to death of heretics

The Interpreter

Did he dream of finding descendants of the Lost
Tribes in Asia—Jewish traders in spices, slaves,
cotton and gold? According to *mi abuelo*,

Cristovao Colon chose Luis de Torres, (born
Yosef ben HaLevi Halvri), as interpreter
for the voyage because he spoke Hebrew.

Where were the silk-clad merchants and sages
they expected to discover? The Great Khan of China?
Marco Polo's Japan of gold palaces, red pearls?

Confusing West Indies for the East, Colon sent
de Torres and a sailor ashore when they reached
Guanahani to meet the ruler of *los Indios*.

Stories passed down like heirlooms had de Torres
greeting the *cacique* with open arms: *Shalom aleichem,
we come as friends bearing gifts.*

Speaking only Taino, the chief honored them with food
and presents. De Torres gestured to convey his desire
for gold. Pointing to native nose rings and amulets,

offering small trinkets in trade, the interpreter
pursued Colon's quest for riches, the *converso*
vow to find safe haven for the Jews.

He and the sailor marveled as *tukkis* wandered
the island, natives smoked tobacco through their noses,
slept in hammocks, paddled their canoes.

Abuelo says de Torres and others were left behind
to set up La Navidad, later burned to the ground when
sailors mistreated the women, behaved like beasts.

Guanahani (Taino)—named San Salvador by Colon
cacique (Sp)—chief

Shalom aleichem (Heb)—peace be upon you, greeting
tukkis (Sp)—turkeys
La Navidad (Sp)—(Nativity), colony founded by Colon

Pirate, Rabbi, Diplomat, Spy

The ship of Samuel sailed from the *mellah* of Fez, captained by Rabbi Palache. Black scarf draped around his head, phoenix carved into his chest.

Abuelo tells us this bird of myth, reborn from ashes, is like our truth, indestructible, even in rabid faith's fire.

Crewed by *conversos*, a kosher chef, this ship shifted shape near Spanish galleons, captured arms and spices for trade, swallowed the tongues of Catholic sailors.

The Barbary coast, a wily maiden, was lover to pirates and thieves, the realm of Sultans, skullduggery, a treasury of stories we stay up to hear.

Far from Torah and Talmud, Palache could don an envoy's cloak, dance the waltz of diplomats in Europe's halls of hypocrisy, navigate rooms of serpents, soothsayers—

their bellies filled with Sephardic ballads, wine made from widow's bones. He carried the names of the expelled and exiled—salted to preserve yet sweet on his lips.

No draughts of amnesia to weaken his sorrow. No lighting of candles, supplications to saints. No surrender.

Magus of myth, Palache wore danger as a suit of feathers, laughed at his enemies, played one ruler against the other. Never sang the hymn of the martyr.

Though kin to luck, brother of lizard, he was set up and captured as a pirate in England, but then let go. Outraged, a Spanish ambassador, inflated like pig's bladder, complained that Jews were favored over Christians. A Protestant official reminded the ambassador, *But sir, Spaniards don't distinguish Englishmen and Jews—they burn both the same.*

mellah (Heb)—Jewish ghetto

Double Wedding

Mi hermana Rosa and I feel like ghosts in petticoats
as we dress for the public wedding, our piety
in place like makeup we'll wash off tonight
and replace in the morning. *Abuelita's* pearls
adorn my neck like worry beads,
my wedding shoes are filled with stones.
Fear, the dry *acequia*, runs through each
room of the house—my family and I,
pawns in a deadly game of hide and seek.

Yesterday as dusk descended, the true marriage
joined two hearts and families in uncertain joy.
Windows closed against the curious, *mi esposo*
and I fasted then prayed, our hands bound
together with white cloth. A simple meal from
the same plate: tortilla, apple, bitter herbs
and honey, wine from the same silver
vessel, we vowed to honor the law
of *El Moises*, heritage of awe and terror.

Now we must enter church as *los novios* anew,
my mask of forgetting held in place by an embroidered
rebozo, my love an unspoken prayer. I will say
the rosary for *Santa Esterika* as I dream of roses
blossoming as grace, of children unburdened
by lineage, by the need to not see what
they see. The strain of charade on this day
of sweets and ashes, eased only by familiar faces,
my devotion to *HaShem* and *mi esposo*, Miguel.

---

mi hermana (Sp)—my sister
acequia (Sp)—irrigation ditch
mi esposo (Sp)—my husband
los novios (Sp)—engaged couple
rebozo (Sp)—shawl
HaShem (Heb)—God

Sub Rosa

The same dream:
It is raining blue cornflowers
and yellow *rosas de castilla*.
There are two roads before me,
both strewn with rocks and peril—
one with a cross on top of a boulder,
the other with a sword amidst pomegranates
and cinders from the fires of faith.
I wake before I can choose a path—
to a cinnamon and saffron sunrise,
and in my true name, Raquel, recite
the *Modeh Ani,* thanking *HaShem*
for restoring my soul.

Grateful for this day yet aware
of its danger, of snakes under chairs,
of devil's weed, I make tortillas, throw
the first one away in offering, and think
of the moon. Remembering what *Abuelita*
told me, how envy and greed fuel the *autos de fe,*
I resume my public face and name—Isabel—
for my friend Maria's visit. *Never outshine
your neighbors or friends, become still water
with hidden depths, Abuelita* would say
as she blessed me. Now I must put my
colcha away, the one I've embroidered
with angels and six-pointed roses.

---

rosas de castilla (Sp)—Persian roses brought by Spanish colonists to New Mexico
Modeh Ani (Heb)—Jewish morning prayer
colcha (Sp)—coverlet

Los Marranos

> *The Lord said to Moses and Aaron, "Say to the Israelites: 'Of all the animals that live on land, these are the ones you may eat: You may eat any animal that has a divided hoof and that chews the cud.'" Leviticus 11:1—47*

I don't like pigs. We keep them
in the yard to help maintain
our *fachada* but never eat them.
Madrecita says, *no es limpio.*

Truly, I find them disgusting.
Snorting, snuffling, squeaking—
snouts rooting in dirt, foraging
in our garden. I avoid them.

Yet my identity is sullied
by association. The ignorant,
the Inquisitors, refer to us, the hidden
ones, as *marranos*, filthy swine.

Strange since they accuse us
of bathing too often, watch to see
if we change linens and clothes
on Fridays as if cleanliness is a sin.

Sometimes I dwell in the between
world, half in dream, half in one reality
or another, my only anchor, *mi familia.*
My solace, a secret prayer inside the foot

of the Madonna. I kiss my fingers
and touch the Virgin on my way out
the door. And yearn for the day
I can live undivided.

―――――――
los marranos (Sp)—swine
no es limpio (Sp)—not clean

When to Do Nothing

The desert has taken my voice.

Chewing on shadows, moonlight strews
white-gold leaves before a chapel
of sand and bones that speak for me.

Bright things rest easy in sky's wake.

I mourn the unthinkable, stories and lineage
lost through fear of persecution, pray
for the wisdom of when to do nothing.

Fruiting grape vines find a way to climb,
steal sunlight from piñon and cottonwood,
then share branches with larks and lizards.

There is always room for the unimagined.

Autumn Sabbath

> *Blessed is the one who does not walk in step*
> *with the wicked.... Psalm 1*

In this waning season, a last
burn of amber and gold bathes
mi abuelo in *la luz divina*.
La Morada, guardian of secrets
within secrets, will be his refuge
as three stars bless night's sky.

Abuelo wears his life like the *tallit*
beneath his coat, ragged,
cherished—all but invisible
except to the chosen—
and his hat, indoors and out—
to honor *HaShem*.

Bowed by two faces of piety,
he seeks solace in the not-two
as he makes his way slowly
to the gathering place; his shadow,
a long crow feather, floats
on leafy wings of *Malachim*.

Dweller in *dos mundos: penitente—*
converso, Manuel and Moises,
he is devoted only to *El Dio*.
On this night, risking all, *mi abuelo*
will cover the *santos*, put flame to candles
and pray in his soul's native tongue.

---

la luz divina (Sp)—divine light
La Morada (Sp)—Penitente chapel
tallit (Heb)—prayer shawl
Malachim (Heb)—angels/messengers of God
dos mundos (Sp)—two worlds

Unborn Reveries

There are days when wind lifts my burdens
and I weep with happiness. When I forget
to remember why I must remain wary.

Lying naked under covers, my ripening belly
is the world, its cherished fruit, the seed of
aspiration for *mi esposo, mi familia, mi gente*.

I am certain I will birth a boy. My dreams
are filled with his laughter as he flies
through *la casa*, his eyes like two suns.

I have heard the river call his name: Rafael,
Rafael. Felt his tiny feet within me soft
as butterfly's wing flutter.

I can sense his impatience, braided through
my own, push against fears for his future.
And hope. A vase of mixed flowers and thorns.

Soon he will insist I let him go, leaving a dark
well of uncertainty. Will my love be enough
to seal his safety?

---

mi gente (Sp)—my people
la casa (Sp)—house

The Birth

I was the Red Sea parting,
feared I would be battered
and bloodied. *La partera* sat
behind me solid as cedar, hands
kneading my swollen belly.
Madrecita wiped my brow
and whispered, *Mija, tener
coraje. Mi parto* seemed endless,
receding then progressing until
I was carried on a tidal wave
of nearly unbearable intensity
to birth my son.

When it was over, I held him
to my breast, flooded with love.
Went through the rituals
and celebrations in a blur: baptism
followed by cleansing his head
to undo the Catholic rite, prayers
for a guardian angel, a symbolic slit
in *Mijo's* foreskin on the eighth
day to mark the covenant
between God and our people.
None of it registered. I had eyes
and heart only for Rafael.

La partera (Sp)—midwife
Mija, tener coraje (Sp)—my daughter, have courage
parto (Sp)—labor
Mijo (Sp)—my son

Remembering Mi Abuelo

The scar on *La Culebra's* belly runs
serpentine across the bloodstained
landscape, lightning rod for a woman's pain.

Behind closed curtains I helped stitch his shroud
with prayers and silk thread, then covered the mirrors.
Thick walls in my grandparents' house absorbed our sorrow.

As we mourned, we remembered: the sound of morning
prayers in the hidden room—music to feed the *neshama*,
the laughing bells on *Abuelo's* horse, the light in his eyes.

His tears of rage when he told us of jackals and rogues
cloaked as friars who blackmailed his brothers with threats
of *autos de fe*, his tears of sadness when his only son died.

I have come to *La Culebra* to honor *Abuelo*, to place
a stone on his grave—stones upon stones,
stars within crosses, a small open book of life.

At sunset, the hills are mauve and rough
carnelian; my children play and hide amidst
gravestones and garter snakes at the *camposanto*.

On moon-blessed evenings like this, when sage gleams
silver and sparrows surrender to sleep, I remember the family
stories he shared that kept us awake and determined to triumph.

La Culebra (Sp)—(harmless snake), mountain peak near San Luis, New Mexico
neshama (Heb)—soul
camposanto (Sp)—cemetery

Prayers to Be Inscribed in the Book of Life for another Year

Again we bury our intentions
by the *acequia* that runs along our fields.
To anyone watching, we seem to be picking
spinach. It is *Yom Kippur*. From dawn to sunset,
we fast and pray, seeking forgiveness. A day
of self-reflection, atonement. A day to turn
the soil with *kavanah*.

My father's face is lit by devotion's fire,
weathered the way a mountain flexes
and contracts with the stress of holding
firm against storms, shifting currents.
Eyes of copper flecked with steel
find innocence in a desert landscape,
joy at a daughter's song.

If *Madrecita* is the anchor of our family, *Padrecito*
is both rudder and sail. He steers a course
around *padres* and politics, trying to protect us
from the ire of Inquisitors, *mal de ojo* of envious
neighbors. He dreams of *Eretz Israel*, life
without guile. Pain rides beside him as we
head home at sunset to break the fast.

Yom Kippur (Heb)—Day of Atonement, holiest day of the year in Judaism
kavanah (Heb)—intention
mal de ojo (Sp)—evil eye
Eretz Israel (Heb)—Greater Israel, land of Israel

Kaddish

Mi esposo wanders the mesa finding solace on the rim of moonless night.
Miguel, born of conquistadors, bears secrets whispered only in the night.

Along the Rio Grande, he hears the *shofar* of his ancestors calling him to pray.
Fragments of psalms passed through *la sangre*, he recites before bed each night.

How can he wear two faces without confusion or regret? Without giving himself away?
His heart is weighed down by the santos he turns toward the wall each night.

His *neshama*, veiled by piety, outward devotion to Catholic rite, longs to be free.
I offer him a continent of stars and succor, as we come together to love at night.

As *rezador*, he must guard the sacred texts, remember the proverbs and prayers.
He will stand with the men in a hidden room as they *daven* on *Shabbos* night.

During the day, he mingles, oil and water, with the trinity: culture, politics, religion.
Bird of prey, he must watch for snakes and scorpions, relaxing vigilance only at night.

Where is the grace in the Edict of Grace? Why does blood drip from wings of tolerance?
Miguel writes our history with his boot in the sand, cries out his sorrow to the night.

Eyes toward Jerusalem, he prays for a world he believes was meant to be.
Déjame morir y ser enterrado como un Judío: his last words echo through the night.

Kaddish (Heb)—memorial prayer
shofar (Heb)—ram's horn
la sangre (Sp)—blood
rezador (Heb)—prayer leader
daven (Heb)—pray
Shabbos (Heb)—Sabbath
Déjame morir y ser enterrado como un judío (Sp)—Let me die and be buried as a Jew

Cara Vemos, Corazón no Concemos

> *Even though we see the face, we cannot know*
> *what is in the heart (Spanish saying)*

Josefina's innocence, balm for terrifying
thoughts and omens, fills me with the scent
of peaches and juniper. *Mija's* face, unmarked
by the bride of despair, reflects what is wholesome
and holy. Somehow, she knows her own soul.

I watch her flourish, wish I could enfold her
in eagle wings, fly her to an aerie in *Eretz Israel*.
But we are rooted in sixteen hundred's
Nuevo Mexico, exiled from our true home,
refugees from the avarice of fanatics' fires.

As mother, what can I offer? Following me,
a duckling imprinted, she can cook, embroider
and sing for her father, plant tomatoes
and squash near sage and chamisa. Sense
when to question and when to stay silent.

This season of snow and shadow, she turns twelve—
time to reveal what's been hidden: *Kiddush* cup,
Shabbos candles, the breath of *Shekinah*.
Two words *somos Judiós* spell the death
of her childhood. Still, she laughs at the future.

Kiddush cup (Heb)—special cup for blessing wine on sabbath or Jewish holidays
Shekinah (Heb)—Divine Presence, feminine attributes of the presence of God
somos Judios (Sp)—we are Jews

Suggested Readings

Adler, Joseph. *Christopher Columbus' Voyage of Discovery: Jewish and New Christian Elements.* Midstream 43: 25 November 1998. http://www.saudades.org/ccolumbusvoyage.html

Baca, Ray Michael. *Brotherhood of the Light.* Mountainview, CA: Floricante Press, 2005.

Bronitsky, Gordon, Ph.D. *Solomon Bibo: Jew and Indian at Acoma Pueblo.* Southwest Jewish Archives.

Brooks, Andree. *Jewish Recipes of the Inquisition.* New York Times Archives, April 16, 1997.

Calado, Carlos. *Behind the Myth, Beyond the Legend, Christopher Columbus, Discoverer of America was Portugese.* —Núcleo de Amigos da Cuba, Jan. 2005 http://amigosdacuba.no.sapo.pt/paginas/p16-christopher_columbus.htm

Carvajal, Doreen. *The Forgetting River.* New York, NY: Riverhead Books, 2012.

da Silva, Manuel Luciano, M. D.. *Columbus was 100% Portuguese!* www.dightonrock.com/columbus_was_100_portuguese.htm

http://dnaconsultants.com/_blog/DNA_Consultants_Blog/post/Signs_of_Crypto-Jewish_Heritage/

http://www.geni.com/projects/Crypto-Jews-Conversos-Marranos-Anusim/8486

Gedalyahu, Tzvi Ben. *Christopher Columbus, Voyages to the New World.* Arutz Sheva 7, Israelnationalnews.com

Gershon, Chaim. *Kabbalistic Signet Indicates Columbus was an Exiled Jew, Luis de Torres.* Avakesh, April 4, 2010. http://www.avakesh.com/2010/04/luis-de-torres.html

Gitlitz, David M.. *The Lost Minyan.* Albuquerque, NM: University of

New Mexico Press, 2010.

Gutierrez, Rabbi Juan Bejarano. *The Religion of Spanish and Portuguese Jews*. Apuntes: Reflexiones teologicas desde el contexto Hispano-Latino,Year 31, No 1, 2011.

Hernández, Frances. *The Secret Jews of the Southwest*, p. 411-454. http://americanjewisharchives.org/publications/journal/PDF/1992_44_01_00_hernandez.pdf

Herz, Cary. *New Mexico's Crypto-Jews: Images and Memory*. Albuquerque, NM: University of New Mexico Press, 2007.

Hoffman, Michael . *The Real Meaning of Yom Kippur*. henry makow.com, September 13, 2013.

Hordes, Stanley M.. *To the End of the Earth*. New York, NY: Columbia University Press, 2005.

Jacobovici. Simcha. *Fernando Torres, Jews and Christopher Columbus*. The Blogs, The Times of Israel, http://blogs.timesofisrael.com/fernando-torres-jews-and-christopher-columbus/#ixzz3IzfBGJM9.

Jacobs, Janet Liebman. *Women Ritual and Secrecy: The Creation of Crypto-Jewish Culture*. Journal for the Scientific Study of Religion, http://www.jstor.org/stable/10.2307/i260036. Vol. 35, No. 2, June,1996, p. 97-108.

Jacobson, Judie. *Columbus Day? Cristóvão Colón, a Portuguese Sephardic Jew, discovered America*. Connecticut Jewish Ledger, Oct 9, 2013

Jones, Douglas W. *The Jews of 1632*. Submission for the Grantville Gazette

Kritzler, Edward. *Jewish Pirates of the Caribbean*. New York, NY: Anchor Books, 2009.

Kritzler, Edward. *Oy-yuy-yuy & a bottle of Schnaps.* The United Congregation of Israelites, Kingston, Jamaica, Jan. 13 http://www.ucija.org/?p=13.

Kunin, Seth D. *The Secret Jews of New Mexico.* Reform Judaism magazine, the Union of American Hebrew Congregations, Summer 2001 http://uahc.org/rjmag/

Kunin, Seth D.. *Juggling Identities.* New York, NY: Columbia University Press, 2009.

Lazar, Moshe. *Scorched Parchments and Tortured Memories: The "Jewishness" of the Anussim (Crypto-Jews)*, p176-199, "Cultural Encounters: The Impact of the Inquisition in Spain and the New World," international conference, University of California, Los Angeles and the University of Southern California, March 25, 26, and 27, 1988,

Levine, Yitzchok. Luis de Carvajal, Jr.: *In the Clutches of the Inquisition.* Department of Mathematical Sciences Stevens Institute of Technology Hoboken, NJ 07030. llevine@stevens.edu

Martinez, Mario X.. *Converso.* Gaon Books, 2012.

Melammed, Renee Levine. *"Conversas." Jewish Women: A Comprehensive Historical Encyclopedia.* 1 March 2009.

Jewish Women's Archive. http://jwa.org/encyclopedia/article/conversas.

Minster, Christopher. *La Navidad: First European Settlement in the Americas.* about.com

Mock, Robert. *The Mystery of the Date Christopher Columbus set Sail to Find the Land of India.* Destination Yisra'el: A Blog for the Lost Ten Tribers Awakening to Their New Reality, 02/13/201. http://destination-yisrael.biblesearchers.com/destination-yisrael/2011/02/the-mystery-of-the-date-christopher-columbus-set-sail-to-find-the-land-of-india.html.

Ross, Theodore. *Shalom on the Range: In Search of the American Crypto-Jew.* Harper's Magazine, Decmber, 2009.

Round, Simon. *Is this the real-life Jewish pirate who inspired Johnny Depp?* The Jewish Chronicle Online, June 25, 2009

Sandoval, Isabelle Medina. *Guardians of Hidden Traditions.* Gaon Books, 2009.

St John History. *The Tainos & the Search for Gold in the New World.* http://seestjohn.com/history_gold.html

Tobias, Henry J. *A History of the Jews in New Mexico.* Albuquerque, NM: University of New Mexico Press, 1990.

Tomás, José Pardo. *Physicians' and Inquisitors' Stories? Circumcision and Crypto-Judaism in Sixteenth-Eighteenth-Century Spain,* Ch 8, p 168-194.

Ward, Seth. https://drsethward.wordpress.com/2012/10/17/profiles-of-converso-descendants-in-the-south/. *Profiles of Converso Descendants in the Southwest U.S.: Manito, Marrano, Sephardic and Jewish Identities among the Crypto-Jews of contemporary New Mexico and Southern Colorado.* Revised version of a paper presented to the Society for Crypto-Jewish Studies, meeting in Los Angeles, CA, August 8, 1999.

http://www.Vistamagazine.com/. VISTA Magazine; http://www.flmnh.ufl.edu/. Florida Museum of Natural History *Did Your Family Sail with Columbus?* July 7, 1991.

Wheelwright, Jeff. *The Wandering Gene and the Indian Princess.* New York, NY:W. W. Norton & Company, 2012.

Wikipedia, the free encyclopedia. *Samuel Pallache.*

Wordsmith, Paula Rose. *Was Christopher Columbus a Sephardic Jew?*

Year of 5,000 Books. http://paulawordsmith.blogspot.com/2011/07/was-christopher-columbus-sephardic-jew.html

Carol Alena Aronoff, Ph.D. is a psychologist, teacher and poet who co-founded SAGE, a psycho-spiritual program for elders; helped guide a Tibetan Buddhist Meditation center for seven years and taught Holistic Health: Eastern Perspectives; Imagery, Meditation and Healing; and Women's Holistic Health at San Francisco State University for nearly fourteen years. She guided Healing in Nature retreats in Hawaii and the Southwest, had a counseling practice and was a Reiki practitioner in Marin County, CA, for many years as well as a volunteer in the program at Marin General Hospital offering imagery sessions to patients and staff. She co-authored *Practical Buddhism: The Kagyu Path* with Ole Nydahl in 1989, edited five books and four meditation booklets on Tibetan Buddhism and published a textbook: *Compassionate Healing: Eastern Perspectives* in 1992.

Her poetry has been published in *Comstock Review, Potpourri, Poetic Realm, Poetica, Mindprints, Beginnings, Hawaii Island Journal, In Our Own Words, Theater of the Mind, Animals in Poetry, From the Web, HeartLodge, Out of Line, Sendero, Buckle &, Iodine, Asphodel, Tiger's Eye, Nomad's Choir, Cyclamens & Swords, Tale Spinners, Poet's Lane, The New Verse News, Kaleidoscope, Radix, Expressing Bridges, Quill & Parchment, Lilipoh, Avocet., Bosque, Zingara, Pyrokinection, Jellyfish Whispers, The Ghazal Page, Origami, Sourland Review, Vox Poetica, The Wild Word, Writing for Peace, Panoply, Novice Writer, Nightingale and Sparrow, The Beautiful Space, Nature Writing, Amethyst, Minute Magazine, Event Horizon, Young Ravens, Otherwise Engaged, Writing in a Woman's Voice, Foreign Lit, Total Eclipse* and *Verse of Silence.*

Her poems have also appeared in numerous anthologies: *Out of Line, 200 New Mexico Poems, Voices Israel, Women Write Resistance, Before There is Nowhere to Stand, Malala: Poems for Malala Yousafzai, The Four Seasons, Poetry of the American Southwest, Secrets/Dreams, Shattered, Tranquility, Dove Tales: Empathy in Art: Embracing the Other, Jeté Away* and *Without Words.*

She received a prize in the 1999/2000 *Common Ground* spiritual poetry contest, judged by Jane Hirshfield, and was twice nominated for a Pushcart Prize. She won the *Tiger's Eye* contest on the writing life and has participated a number of times in *Braided Lives*, a collaboration of artists and poets as well as in SKEA's *Art and Nature event, Ekphrasis: Sacred Stories of the Southwest*, and *(A) Muses Poster Retrospective* for the 2014 Taos Fall Arts Festival. She judged the 2008 Tiger's Eye poetry contest.

Cornsilk, a chapbook of poems about Hopi and Hawaii, was published by Indian Heritage Council in 2004, and her illustrated poetry book, *The Nature of Music*, was published by Pelican Pond/Blue Dolphin Publishing in 2005. An expanded, illustrated *Cornsilk* was published in 2006, *Her Soup Made the Moon Weep*, in 2007 and *Blessings from an Unseen World* in 2013. *Dreaming Earth's Body: poems by Carol Alena Aronoff, paintings by Betsie Miller-Kusz* was published by Blue Dolphin in 2015. Her sixth full-length poetry book, *The Gift of Not Finding: Poems for Meditation*, is forthcoming in 2020 from Homestead Lighthouse Press.

Currently, Carol Aronoff resides in a rural area of Hawaii—working her land, meditating in nature and writing.